Piano • Vocal • Guitar

Last Christmas

MUSIC FROM THE MOTION PICTURE SOUNDTRACK

FEATURING THE MUSIC OF
George Michael and Wham!

ISBN 978-1-5400-8271-8

HAL•LEONARD®

Visit Hal Leonard Online at
www.halleonard.com

Contact us:
Hal Leonard
7777 West Bluemound Road
Milwaukee, WI 53213
Email: info@halleonard.com

In Europe, contact:
Hal Leonard Europe Limited
42 Wigmore Street
Marylebone, London, W1U 2RN
Email: info@halleonardeurope.com

In Australia, contact:
Hal Leonard Australia Pty. Ltd.
4 Lentara Court
Cheltenham, Victoria, 3192 Australia
Email: info@halleonard.com.au

CONTENTS

4 **Last Christmas**

10 **Too Funky**

22 **Fantasy**

17 **Praying for Time**

32 **Faith**

37 **Waiting for That Day**

48 **Heal the Pain**

66 **One More Try**

57 **Fastlove, Pt. 1**

70 **Everything She Wants**

83 **Wake Me Up Before You Go-Go**

76 **Move On**

95 **Freedom! 90**

88 **This Is How (We Want You to Get High)**

LAST CHRISTMAS

Words and Music by
GEORGE MICHAEL

Once bit - ten and twice shy, _____
A crowd - ed room, friends with tired ____ eyes. ____

I keep my dis - tance but tears still catch ____ my eye. ____
I'm hid - ing from you and your soul ____ of ice. ____

TOO FUNKY

Words and Music by
GEORGE MICHAEL

(Gon - na be the kind of lov - er that you nev - er had.) Hey, you're just to funk - y. ___

(You're nev - er gon - na have an - oth - er lov - er in your bed.) You're just too funk - y for me. ___

(Spoken:) Would you like me to seduce you? Is that what you're trying to tell me?

PRAYING FOR TIME

Words and Music by
GEORGE MICHAEL

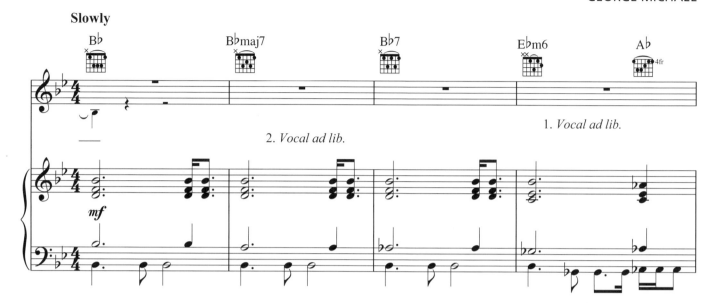

Slowly

2. *Vocal ad lib.*

1. *Vocal ad lib.*

mf

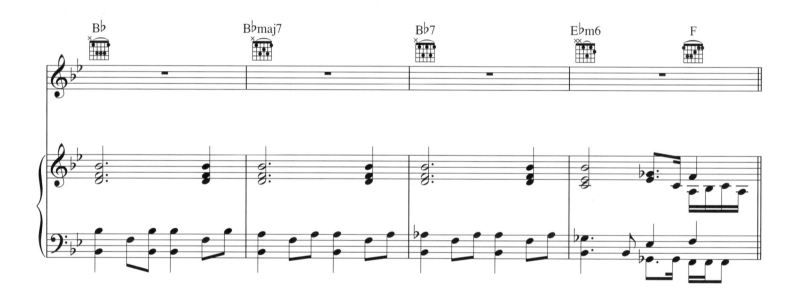

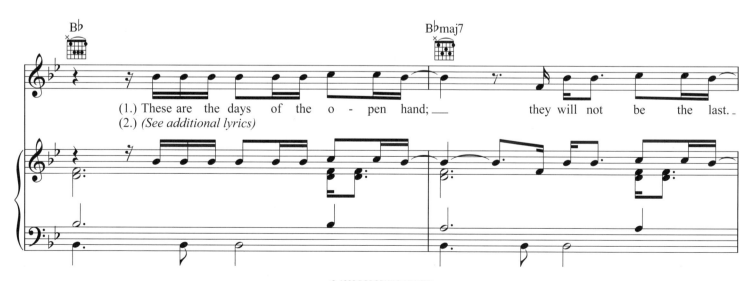

(1.) These are the days of the o - pen hand; ___ they will not be the last. ___
(2.) *(See additional lyrics)*

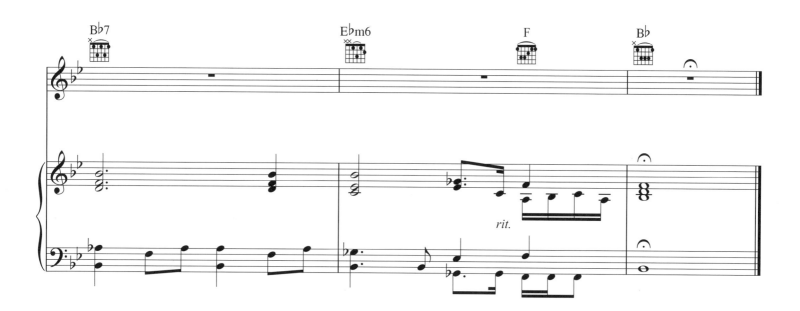

Additional Lyrics

2. These are the days of the empty hand;
Oh, you hold on to what you can
And charity is a coat you wear twice a year.
This is the year of the guilty man;
Your television takes a stand
And you find that what was over there is over here.
So you scream from behind your door, say what's mine is mine and not yours.
I may have too much, but I'll take my chances
'Cause God's stopped keeping score.
And you cling to the things they sold you.
Did you cover your eyes when they told you
That he can't come back 'cause he has no children to come back for?
To Chorus

FANTASY

Words and Music by
GEORGE MICHAEL

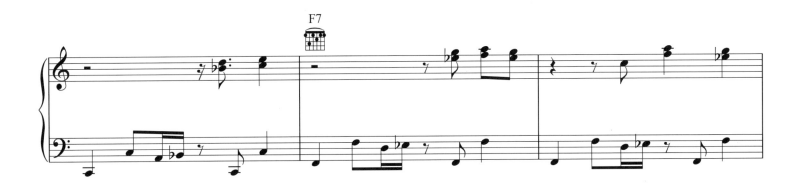

Recorded a half step lower.

One day you say you love __ me, the
One day you make me feel __ that your

next you tell __ me you don't.
love is in _____ my hands.

One day you say you will, __ the
One day you say you'll stay, __ the

Instrumental solo ad lib.

Solo ends You hang a - round with peo - ple who are

FAITH

Words and Music by
GEORGE MICHAEL

Brightly, with a beat

Well, I guess it would be nice

Instrumental
by,

if I ____ could

I know ____ you're

touch your bod - y.
ask - ing me ____ to stay.

I know not ev - 'ry - bod - y
Say please, please, please don't go ____ a - way.

has got a bod - y like you. ____
You say I'm giv - ing you the blues. ____

Oh,
May - be

but I got - ta think
be

twice   be - fore ___ I   give   my   heart ___ a - way.
you mean   ev - 'ry   word ___ you say.

And   I   know   all   the   games ___ you play   be - cause   I   play   them
Can't   help   but   think   of   yes - ter - day   and   an - oth - er   who

too. ___   Oh,   but   I   need   some ___ time ___
tied   me   down   to   the   lov - er - boy   rules. }
Instrumental ends }   Be -   fore   this ___ riv -

___ off   from   that   e -   mo -   tion, _____
- er   be -   comes   an ___ o -   cean, ___   be -

WAITING FOR THAT DAY

Words and Music by GEORGE MICHAEL,
MICK JAGGER and KEITH RICHARDS

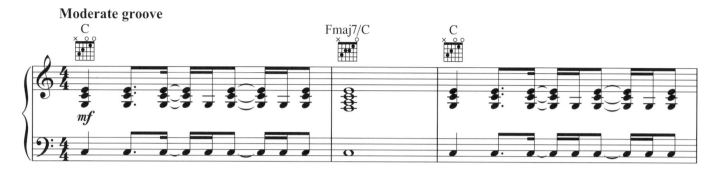

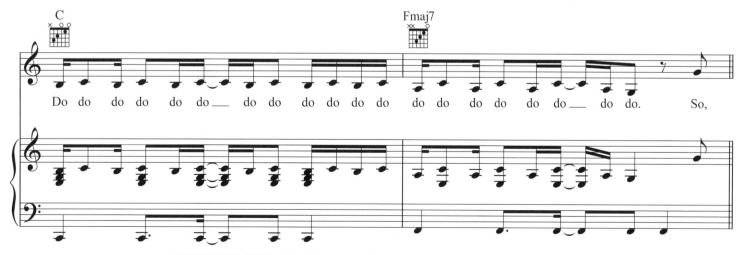

HEAL THE PAIN

Words and Music by
GEORGE MICHAEL

Do do do, ____ do do do do, ____ do do do do ____ do do ____ do do do. ____ Do do do do, ____

FASTLOVE

Words and Music by GEORGE MICHAEL,
PATRICE RUSHEN, TERRI McFADDIN
and FREDDIE WASHINGTON

ONE MORE TRY

Words and Music by
GEORGE MICHAEL

Additional Lyrics

2. When you were just a stranger and I was at your feet,
   I didn't feel the danger, now I feel the heat.
   That look in your eyes telling me no
   So you think that you love me, know that you need me.
   I wrote the song. I know it's wrong, just let me go. *(To Chorus)*

(D.S.) And, teacher, there are things that I still have to learn.
   But the one thing I have is my pride. Oh, so I don't wanna learn to
   Hold you, touch you, think that you're mine,
   Because there ain't no joy for an uptown boy who just isn't willing to try.
   I'm so cold inside.
   (To Coda)

EVERYTHING SHE WANTS

Words and Music by
GEORGE MICHAEL

Medium Rock

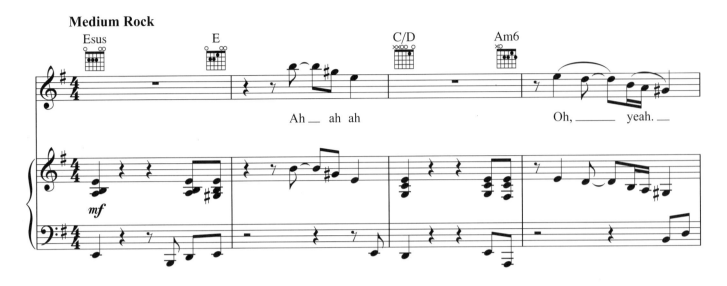

Ah __ ah ah   Oh, _____ yeah. __

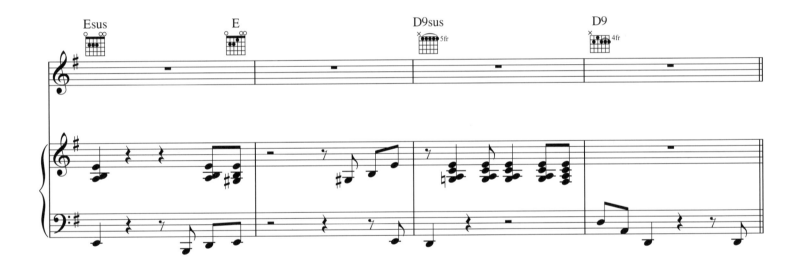

Some - bod - y told __ me,   boy, ev - 'ry - thing she wants   is

MOVE ON

Words and Music by
GEORGE MICHAEL

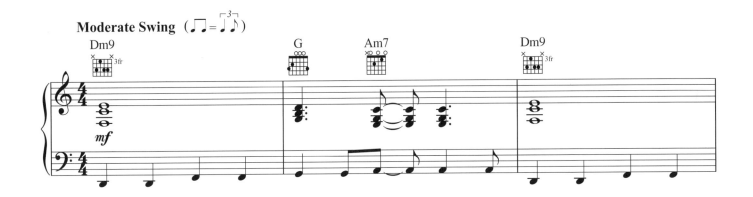

I've been in _____ and out of fa - vor with
I've been in _____ and out of fa - vor with

la - dy _____ luck. _____ I've got - ta tell you that   I've _____ seen things _____
love be - cause _____ I've got - ta tell you that   I've _____ been things _____

WAKE ME UP BEFORE YOU GO-GO

Words and Music by
GEORGE MICHAEL

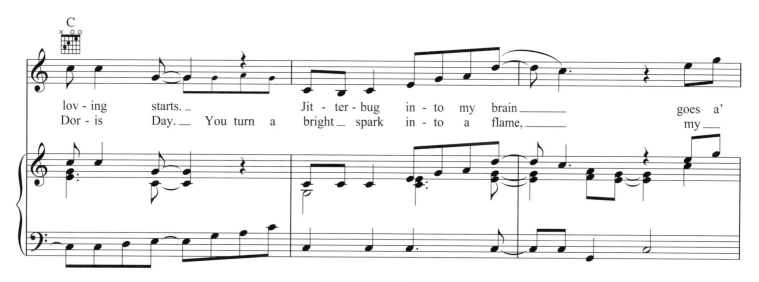

THIS IS HOW
(We Want You to Get High)

Words and Music by GEORGE MICHAEL
and JAMES JACKMAN

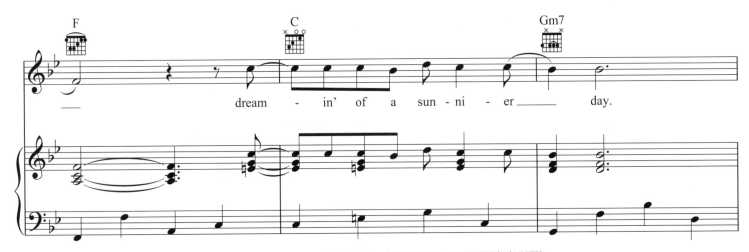

FREEDOM '90

Words and Music by
GEORGE MICHAEL

Moderately

I ___ won't let ___ you down; __ I will _ not give _ you up, _

__ got to have _ some faith _ in the sound. _ It's the one _ good thing _ that I've

got. I ___ won't let ___ you down. ___ So please _ don't give _ me up, _

'cause I ___ would real - ly, real - ly love ___ to stick a-round,   oh

yeah. __ *(Vocal 1st time only)*

Heav-en knows__ I was__   just a young boy,   did-n't know what I want-ed to be,__
Heav-en knows__ we sure__   had some fun, boy.   What a kick, just a bud-dy and me.__